Manifesting a Legacy

Turning thoughts into actions while creating a life of overflow and abundance.

Printed in the USA by A2Z Books, LLC. Copyright by Chelsea Guarriello. All rights reserved. This book or any portion thereof may not be reproduced or used in any manner whatsoever without the express written permission of the publisher except for the use of brief quotations in book review Printed in the United Stated.
First Printing ISBN 978-1-943284-65-8
www.A2ZBookspublishing.net

This Planner Belongs to:

_____

_____

This Book was written for my baby Summer Rose Burnett. May you never find yourself feeling lost or without. Use this journal to collect your most intimate thoughts and dreams and use your daily actions to help bring them all to life! The world is yours and you can have anything you desire. Dig deep. Aim high and strive for greatness because the world is yours! I love you Summer!

- Mommy

Before you get started

This Journal is for:
- Aspiring entrepreneurs
- Business oriented people
- Moms who want to live out their dreams
- Money driven people

Manifestation is something that is put into your physical reality through thought, feelings, and beliefs. This means that whatever you focus on is what you are bringing into your reality. You have to channel your energy in the correct ways if you really want to be successful. This journal will show you different secrets to become anything you want to in life by taking ACTION. You can't just say you want something without actually writing it down and executing a plan. This journal will help you put dream to paper in the right way! Learn to manifest properly and take your life to new heights.

*Don't speak negatively about
yourself, even as a joke.
Your body doesn't know the difference.
Words are energy and cast spells over your life.
That is why it is called spelling.
Change the way you speak about yourself
and you can change your life.
What you are not changing you are also choosing.*

AUTHOR UNKNOWN

1st Quarter

*I think frugality drives innovation, just like other constraints do.
One of the only ways to get out of a tight box is to invent your way out.*

JEFF BEZOS

What Goals Are you Trying to Attain This Quarter?

(A Goal is defined as the object of a person's ambition or effort; an aim or desired result). Here are some examples:
- My goal is to make $10,000 this quarter.
- My goal is to lose 15lbs this quarter.
- My goal is to write a book this quarter.
- My goal is to find a work from home opportunity this quarter.

_____
_____
_____
_____
_____
_____
_____
_____
_____
_____
_____
_____
_____
_____
_____
_____
_____
_____
_____
_____
_____
_____

What steps/action plan do I need to implement these goals?

Here are some examples:
- This quarter I will increase my marketing budget by 10%.
- This quarter I will give up sugar and alcohol.
- This quarter I will spend less time on Instagram and more time writing my book.
- This quarter I will take my free evenings and research work from home opportunities.

What Goals Are you Trying to Attain This Quarter?

(A Goal is defined as the object of a person's ambition or effort; an aim or desired result). Here are some examples:
- My goal is to make $10,000 this quarter.
- My goal is to lose 15lbs this quarter.
- My goal is to write a book this quarter.
- My goal is to find a work from home opportunity this quarter.

_____
_____
_____
_____
_____
_____
_____
_____
_____
_____
_____
_____
_____
_____
_____
_____
_____
_____
_____
_____
_____
_____
_____
_____
_____

What steps/action plan do I need to implement these goals?

Here are some examples:
- This quarter I will increase my marketing budget by 10%.
- This quarter I will give up sugar and alcohol.
- This quarter I will spend less time on Instagram and more time writing my book.
- This quarter I will take my free evenings and research work from home opportunities.

_____
_____
_____
_____
_____
_____
_____
_____
_____
_____
_____
_____
_____
_____
_____
_____
_____
_____
_____
_____
_____
_____

What sacrifices do I have to make to achieve these goals?

(Sacrifice is defined as giving up something for the sake of a better cause.)
Here are some examples:
- I will make my coffee at home instead of buying it at Starbucks this quarter.
- I will meal prep and not go out to eat with my friends this quarter.
- I will deactivate my Instagram page this quarter.
- I will leave for work 30 mins earlier than usual so that I can have more time to research new ways to make money from home. I will do this this 3 x a week.

Month: _____

SUNDAY	MONDAY	TUESDAY	WEDNESDAY

| THURSDAY | FRIDAY | SATURDAY |

Notes

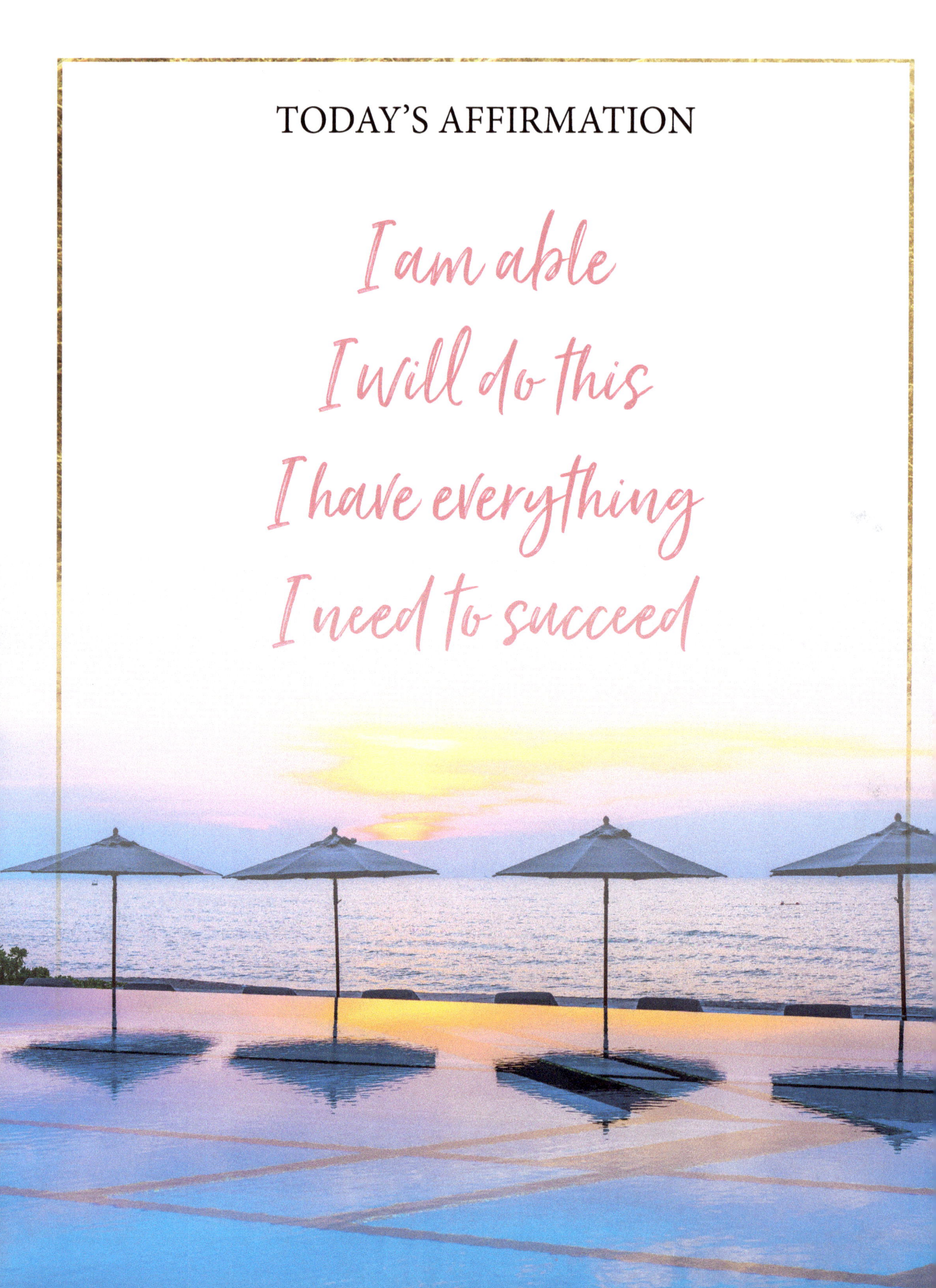

Notes

List of Daily Routines

Having a morning routine assists with developing good habits, which allows us to reach our full potential. Having a morning routine also helps to get rid of distractions and bad habits.

- ✓ Wake up early
- ✓ Meditate
- ✓ Write down 3 things your grateful for.
- ✓ Go Jogging
- ✓ Before you get out of bed Say 3 affirmations out loud.
- ✓ Drink a cup of coffee
- ✓ Don't Get on Social Media
- ✓ Declutter your room/work area
- ✓ Beat your face/ Get glammed up
- ✓ Play your favorite album
- ✓ Make a delicious breakfast
- ✓ Eat a Healthy Breakfast
- ✓ Set 3 short term goals you want to accomplish this week
- ✓ Do/Begin Yoga
- ✓ Make Your Favorite Tea
- ✓ Go get a massage
- ✓ Groom your nails
- ✓ Take a moment to yourself, have a moment of stillness.
- ✓ Speak one affirmation that is the most important to you.
- ✓ Visualize what you want.
- ✓ Write down your affirmation and carry it with you throughout the day.
- ✓ Listen to a podcast about manifesting
- ✓ Paint or Draw your goal/dream
- ✓ Wake up and take a warm bath with a good smelling candle
- ✓ Read a chapter of your favorite book
- ✓ Do your hair and makeup
- ✓ Pray/meditate to calm your spirit
- ✓ Call a friend and catch up
- ✓ Wake up and take 7 deep breaths, in between the breaths say 7 affirmations.
- ✓ If you're religious, read over 7 bible verses that will inspire the day.
- ✓ Spend time with your family and cook breakfast together

- Waking up early automatically puts you ahead of most people productivity wise. It also you gives you more time to include self-care activities.

- Meditation is extremely important for your mind and body. Meditation helps turn negative emotions to positive emotions and can also be a cleanse.

- Starting your day off with gratitude puts you in a better mood throughout the whole day! Even the people around you will have a more pleasant experience being in your presence.

- Exercising is important because it speeds up metabolism, which makes you healthier and it releases endorphins which make you happy.

- Eating a Healthy Breakfast is critical in giving you a clear mind to start the day's activities.

- Saying your affirmation out loud keeps your manifestation goals on track and integral to your miracle.

- Having still and quiet moments helps to center yourself and get to the pureness of who you truly are.

- Visualizing your goals allows you to see them clearly which allows you to achieve them.

Create a Daily Morning Routine

(Choose 2 per day from list and this should stay the same each week).

Monday Morning Routine: (choose 2 from list)
_____
_____

Tuesday Morning Routine: (choose 2 from list)
_____
_____

Wednesday Morning Routine: (choose 2 from list)
_____
_____

Thursday Morning Routine: (choose 2 from list)
_____
_____

Friday Morning Routine: (choose 2 from list)
_____
_____

Saturday Morning Routine: (choose 2 from list)
_____
_____

Sunday Morning Routine: (choose 2 from list)
_____
_____

Create a Daily Morning Routine

(Choose 2 per day from list and this should stay the same each week).

Monday Morning Routine: (choose 2 from list)
_____
_____

Tuesday Morning Routine: (choose 2 from list)
_____
_____

Wednesday Morning Routine: (choose 2 from list)
_____
_____

Thursday Morning Routine: (choose 2 from list)
_____
_____

Friday Morning Routine: (choose 2 from list)
_____
_____

Saturday Morning Routine: (choose 2 from list)
_____
_____

Sunday Morning Routine: (choose 2 from list)
_____
_____

Create a Daily Morning Routine

(Choose 2 per day from list and this should stay the same each week).

Monday Morning Routine: (choose 2 from list)
_____
_____

Tuesday Morning Routine: (choose 2 from list)
_____
_____

Wednesday Morning Routine: (choose 2 from list)
_____
_____

Thursday Morning Routine: (choose 2 from list)
_____
_____

Friday Morning Routine: (choose 2 from list)
_____
_____

Saturday Morning Routine: (choose 2 from list)
_____
_____

Sunday Morning Routine: (choose 2 from list)
_____
_____

Create a Daily Morning Routine

(Choose 2 per day from list and this should stay the same each week).

Monday Morning Routine: (choose 2 from list)
_____
_____

Tuesday Morning Routine: (choose 2 from list)
_____
_____

Wednesday Morning Routine: (choose 2 from list)
_____
_____

Thursday Morning Routine: (choose 2 from list)
_____
_____

Friday Morning Routine: (choose 2 from list)
_____
_____

Saturday Morning Routine: (choose 2 from list)
_____
_____

Sunday Morning Routine: (choose 2 from list)
_____
_____

Month: _____

SUNDAY	MONDAY	TUESDAY	WEDNESDAY

THURSDAY	FRIDAY	SATURDAY

Notes

Notes

List of Daily Routines

Having a morning routine assists with developing good habits, which allows us to reach our full potential. Having a morning routine also helps to get rid of distractions and bad habits.

- ✓ Wake up early
- ✓ Meditate
- ✓ Write down 3 things your grateful for.
- ✓ Go Jogging
- ✓ Before you get out of bed Say 3 affirmations out loud.
- ✓ Drink a cup of coffee
- ✓ Don't Get on Social Media
- ✓ Declutter your room/work area
- ✓ Beat your face/ Get glammed up
- ✓ Play your favorite album
- ✓ Make a delicious breakfast
- ✓ Eat a Healthy Breakfast
- ✓ Set 3 short term goals you want to accomplish this week
- ✓ Do/Begin Yoga
- ✓ Make Your Favorite Tea
- ✓ Go get a massage
- ✓ Groom your nails
- ✓ Take a moment to yourself, have a moment of stillness.
- ✓ Speak one affirmation that is the most important to you.
- ✓ Visualize what you want.
- ✓ Write down your affirmation and carry it with you throughout the day.
- ✓ Listen to a podcast about manifesting
- ✓ Paint or Draw your goal/dream
- ✓ Wake up and take a warm bath with a good smelling candle
- ✓ Read a chapter of your favorite book
- ✓ Do your hair and makeup
- ✓ Pray/meditate to calm your spirit
- ✓ Call a friend and catch up
- ✓ Wake up and take 7 deep breaths, in between the breaths say 7 affirmations.
- ✓ If you're religious, read over 7 bible verses that will inspire the day.
- ✓ Spend time with your family and cook breakfast together

- Waking up early automatically puts you ahead of most people productivity wise. It also you gives you more time to include self-care activities.

- Meditation is extremely important for your mind and body. Meditation helps turn negative emotions to positive emotions and can also be a cleanse.

- Starting your day off with gratitude puts you in a better mood throughout the whole day! Even the people around you will have a more pleasant experience being in your presence.

- Exercising is important because it speeds up metabolism, which makes you healthier and it releases endorphins which make you happy.

- Eating a Healthy Breakfast is critical in giving you a clear mind to start the day's activities.

- Saying your affirmation out loud keeps your manifestation goals on track and integral to your miracle.

- Having still and quiet moments helps to center yourself and get to the pureness of who you truly are.

- Visualizing your goals allows you to see them clearly which allows you to achieve them.

Create a Daily Morning Routine

(Choose 2 per day from list and this should stay the same each week).

Monday Morning Routine: (choose 2 from list)
_____
_____

Tuesday Morning Routine: (choose 2 from list)
_____
_____

Wednesday Morning Routine: (choose 2 from list)
_____
_____

Thursday Morning Routine: (choose 2 from list)
_____
_____

Friday Morning Routine: (choose 2 from list)
_____
_____

Saturday Morning Routine: (choose 2 from list)
_____
_____

Sunday Morning Routine: (choose 2 from list)
_____
_____

Create a Daily Morning Routine

(Choose 2 per day from list and this should stay the same each week).

Monday Morning Routine: (choose 2 from list)
_____
_____

Tuesday Morning Routine: (choose 2 from list)
_____
_____

Wednesday Morning Routine: (choose 2 from list)
_____
_____

Thursday Morning Routine: (choose 2 from list)
_____
_____

Friday Morning Routine: (choose 2 from list)
_____
_____

Saturday Morning Routine: (choose 2 from list)
_____
_____

Sunday Morning Routine: (choose 2 from list)
_____
_____

Create a Daily Morning Routine

(Choose 2 per day from list and this should stay the same each week).

Monday Morning Routine: (choose 2 from list)
_____
_____

Tuesday Morning Routine: (choose 2 from list)
_____
_____

Wednesday Morning Routine: (choose 2 from list)
_____
_____

Thursday Morning Routine: (choose 2 from list)
_____
_____

Friday Morning Routine: (choose 2 from list)
_____
_____

Saturday Morning Routine: (choose 2 from list)
_____
_____

Sunday Morning Routine: (choose 2 from list)
_____
_____

Create a Daily Morning Routine

(Choose 2 per day from list and this should stay the same each week).

Monday Morning Routine: (choose 2 from list)
_____
_____

Tuesday Morning Routine: (choose 2 from list)
_____
_____

Wednesday Morning Routine: (choose 2 from list)
_____
_____

Thursday Morning Routine: (choose 2 from list)
_____
_____

Friday Morning Routine: (choose 2 from list)
_____
_____

Saturday Morning Routine: (choose 2 from list)
_____
_____

Sunday Morning Routine: (choose 2 from list)
_____
_____

Month: _____

SUNDAY	MONDAY	TUESDAY	WEDNESDAY

THURSDAY	FRIDAY	SATURDAY

Notes

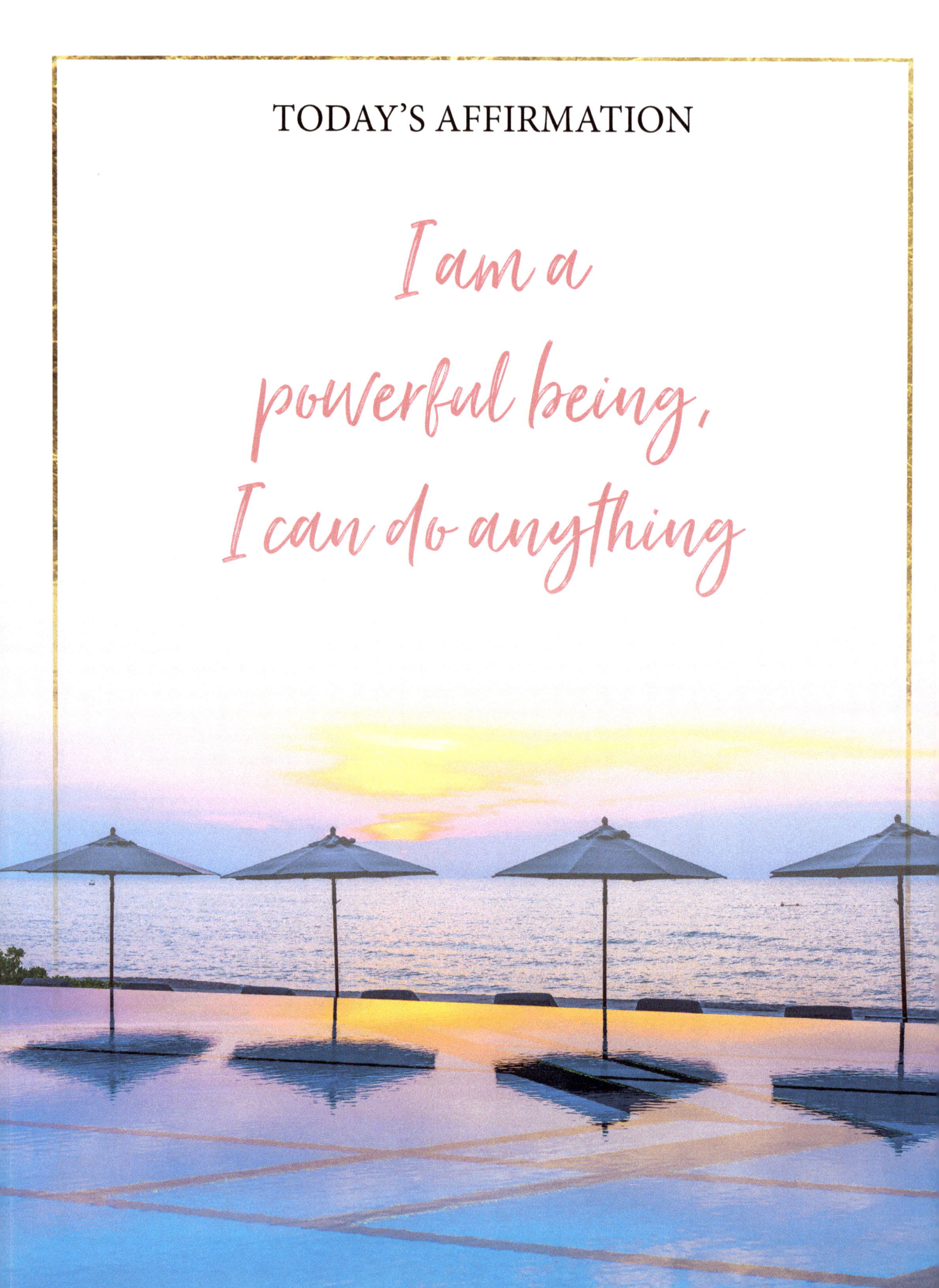

Notes

List of Daily Routines

Having a morning routine assists with developing good habits, which allows us to reach our full potential. Having a morning routine also helps to get rid of distractions and bad habits.

- ✓ Wake up early
- ✓ Meditate
- ✓ Write down 3 things your grateful for.
- ✓ Go Jogging
- ✓ Before you get out of bed Say 3 affirmations out loud.
- ✓ Drink a cup of coffee
- ✓ Don't Get on Social Media
- ✓ Declutter your room/work area
- ✓ Beat your face/ Get glammed up
- ✓ Play your favorite album
- ✓ Make a delicious breakfast
- ✓ Eat a Healthy Breakfast
- ✓ Set 3 short term goals you want to accomplish this week
- ✓ Do/Begin Yoga
- ✓ Make Your Favorite Tea
- ✓ Go get a massage
- ✓ Groom your nails
- ✓ Take a moment to yourself, have a moment of stillness.
- ✓ Speak one affirmation that is the most important to you.
- ✓ Visualize what you want.
- ✓ Write down your affirmation and carry it with you throughout the day.
- ✓ Listen to a podcast about manifesting
- ✓ Paint or Draw your goal/dream
- ✓ Wake up and take a warm bath with a good smelling candle
- ✓ Read a chapter of your favorite book
- ✓ Do your hair and makeup
- ✓ Pray/meditate to calm your spirit
- ✓ Call a friend and catch up
- ✓ Wake up and take 7 deep breaths, in between the breaths say 7 affirmations.
- ✓ If you're religious, read over 7 bible verses that will inspire the day.
- ✓ Spend time with your family and cook breakfast together

- Waking up early automatically puts you ahead of most people productivity wise. It also you gives you more time to include self-care activities.

- Meditation is extremely important for your mind and body. Meditation helps turn negative emotions to positive emotions and can also be a cleanse.

- Starting your day off with gratitude puts you in a better mood throughout the whole day! Even the people around you will have a more pleasant experience being in your presence.

- Exercising is important because it speeds up metabolism, which makes you healthier and it releases endorphins which make you happy.

- Eating a Healthy Breakfast is critical in giving you a clear mind to start the day's activities.

- Saying your affirmation out loud keeps your manifestation goals on track and integral to your miracle.

- Having still and quiet moments helps to center yourself and get to the pureness of who you truly are.

- Visualizing your goals allows you to see them clearly which allows you to achieve them.

Create a Daily Morning Routine

(Choose 2 per day from list and this should stay the same each week).

Monday Morning Routine: (choose 2 from list)
_____
_____

Tuesday Morning Routine: (choose 2 from list)
_____
_____

Wednesday Morning Routine: (choose 2 from list)
_____
_____

Thursday Morning Routine: (choose 2 from list)
_____
_____

Friday Morning Routine: (choose 2 from list)
_____
_____

Saturday Morning Routine: (choose 2 from list)
_____
_____

Sunday Morning Routine: (choose 2 from list)
_____
_____

Create a Daily Morning Routine

(Choose 2 per day from list and this should stay the same each week).

Monday Morning Routine: (choose 2 from list)
_____
_____

Tuesday Morning Routine: (choose 2 from list)
_____
_____

Wednesday Morning Routine: (choose 2 from list)
_____
_____

Thursday Morning Routine: (choose 2 from list)
_____
_____

Friday Morning Routine: (choose 2 from list)
_____
_____

Saturday Morning Routine: (choose 2 from list)
_____
_____

Sunday Morning Routine: (choose 2 from list)
_____
_____

Create a Daily Morning Routine

(Choose 2 per day from list and this should stay the same each week).

Monday Morning Routine: (choose 2 from list)
_____
_____

Tuesday Morning Routine: (choose 2 from list)
_____
_____

Wednesday Morning Routine: (choose 2 from list)
_____
_____

Thursday Morning Routine: (choose 2 from list)
_____
_____

Friday Morning Routine: (choose 2 from list)
_____
_____

Saturday Morning Routine: (choose 2 from list)
_____
_____

Sunday Morning Routine: (choose 2 from list)
_____
_____

Create a Daily Morning Routine

(Choose 2 per day from list and this should stay the same each week).

Monday Morning Routine: (choose 2 from list)
_____
_____

Tuesday Morning Routine: (choose 2 from list)
_____
_____

Wednesday Morning Routine: (choose 2 from list)
_____
_____

Thursday Morning Routine: (choose 2 from list)
_____
_____

Friday Morning Routine: (choose 2 from list)
_____
_____

Saturday Morning Routine: (choose 2 from list)
_____
_____

Sunday Morning Routine: (choose 2 from list)
_____
_____

Am I on track to accomplish the goals I am manifesting?

(If yes what did I do, if no what changes do I need to make?)

Write My Own Affirmation

When you write your affirmations be sure to write them as if they've already shown up in your life! Here are some examples: I LOVE my brand new Range Rover! My new beach home is lavish and beautiful. Perfect for me and my growing family!

_____
_____
_____
_____
_____
_____
_____
_____
_____
_____
_____
_____
_____
_____
_____
_____
_____
_____
_____
_____
_____
_____
_____
_____

If you are born poor it's not your mistake, but if you die poor its your mistake.

BILL GATES

If you don't find a way to make money while you sleep, you will work until you die.

WARREN BUFFET

What Goals Are you Trying to Attain This Quarter?

(A Goal is defined as the object of a person's ambition or effort; an aim or desired result). Here are some examples:
- My goal is to make $10,000 this quarter.
- My goal is to lose 15lbs this quarter.
- My goal is to write a book this quarter.
- My goal is to find a work from home opportunity this quarter.

_____
_____
_____
_____
_____
_____
_____
_____
_____
_____
_____
_____
_____
_____
_____
_____
_____
_____
_____
_____
_____
_____
_____
_____
_____
_____

What steps/action plan do I need to implement these goals?

Here are some examples:
- This quarter I will increase my marketing budget by 10%.
- This quarter I will give up sugar and alcohol.
- This quarter I will spend less time on Instagram and more time writing my book.
- This quarter I will take my free evenings and research work from home opportunities.

What sacrifices do I have to make to achieve these goals?

(Sacrifice is defined as giving up something for the sake of a better cause.)
Here are some examples:
- I will make my coffee at home instead of buying it at Starbucks this quarter.
- I will meal prep and not go out to eat with my friends this quarter.
- I will deactivate my Instagram page this quarter.
- I will leave for work 30 mins earlier than usual so that I can have more time to research new ways to make money from home. I will do this this 3 x a week.

_____
_____
_____
_____
_____
_____
_____
_____
_____
_____
_____
_____
_____
_____
_____
_____
_____
_____
_____
_____
_____
_____
_____
_____

Month: _____

SUNDAY	MONDAY	TUESDAY	WEDNESDAY

THURSDAY	FRIDAY	SATURDAY

Notes

TODAY'S AFFIRMATION

I'm doing the best I can with what I have

Notes

List of Daily Routines

Having a morning routine assists with developing good habits, which allows us to reach our full potential. Having a morning routine also helps to get rid of distractions and bad habits.

- ✓ Wake up early
- ✓ Meditate
- ✓ Write down 3 things your grateful for.
- ✓ Go Jogging
- ✓ Before you get out of bed Say 3 affirmations out loud.
- ✓ Drink a cup of coffee
- ✓ Don't Get on Social Media
- ✓ Declutter your room/work area
- ✓ Beat your face/ Get glammed up
- ✓ Play your favorite album
- ✓ Make a delicious breakfast
- ✓ Eat a Healthy Breakfast
- ✓ Set 3 short term goals you want to accomplish this week
- ✓ Do/Begin Yoga
- ✓ Make Your Favorite Tea
- ✓ Go get a massage
- ✓ Groom your nails
- ✓ Take a moment to yourself, have a moment of stillness.
- ✓ Speak one affirmation that is the most important to you.
- ✓ Visualize what you want.
- ✓ Write down your affirmation and carry it with you throughout the day.
- ✓ Listen to a podcast about manifesting
- ✓ Paint or Draw your goal/dream
- ✓ Wake up and take a warm bath with a good smelling candle
- ✓ Read a chapter of your favorite book
- ✓ Do your hair and makeup
- ✓ Pray/meditate to calm your spirit
- ✓ Call a friend and catch up
- ✓ Wake up and take 7 deep breaths, in between the breaths say 7 affirmations.
- ✓ If you're religious, read over 7 bible verses that will inspire the day.
- ✓ Spend time with your family and cook breakfast together

- Waking up early automatically puts you ahead of most people productivity wise. It also you gives you more time to include self-care activities.

- Meditation is extremely important for your mind and body. Meditation helps turn negative emotions to positive emotions and can also be a cleanse.

- Starting your day off with gratitude puts you in a better mood throughout the whole day! Even the people around you will have a more pleasant experience being in your presence.

- Exercising is important because it speeds up metabolism, which makes you healthier and it releases endorphins which make you happy.

- Eating a Healthy Breakfast is critical in giving you a clear mind to start the day's activities.

- Saying your affirmation out loud keeps your manifestation goals on track and integral to your miracle.

- Having still and quiet moments helps to center yourself and get to the pureness of who you truly are.

- Visualizing your goals allows you to see them clearly which allows you to achieve them.

Create a Daily Morning Routine

(Choose 2 per day from list and this should stay the same each week).

Monday Morning Routine: (choose 2 from list)
_____
_____

Tuesday Morning Routine: (choose 2 from list)
_____
_____

Wednesday Morning Routine: (choose 2 from list)
_____
_____

Thursday Morning Routine: (choose 2 from list)
_____
_____

Friday Morning Routine: (choose 2 from list)
_____
_____

Saturday Morning Routine: (choose 2 from list)
_____
_____

Sunday Morning Routine: (choose 2 from list)
_____
_____

Create a Daily Morning Routine

(Choose 2 per day from list and this should stay the same each week).

Monday Morning Routine: (choose 2 from list)
_____
_____

Tuesday Morning Routine: (choose 2 from list)
_____
_____

Wednesday Morning Routine: (choose 2 from list)
_____
_____

Thursday Morning Routine: (choose 2 from list)
_____
_____

Friday Morning Routine: (choose 2 from list)
_____
_____

Saturday Morning Routine: (choose 2 from list)
_____
_____

Sunday Morning Routine: (choose 2 from list)
_____
_____

Create a Daily Morning Routine

(Choose 2 per day from list and this should stay the same each week).

Monday Morning Routine: (choose 2 from list)
_____
_____

Tuesday Morning Routine: (choose 2 from list)
_____
_____

Wednesday Morning Routine: (choose 2 from list)
_____
_____

Thursday Morning Routine: (choose 2 from list)
_____
_____

Friday Morning Routine: (choose 2 from list)
_____
_____

Saturday Morning Routine: (choose 2 from list)
_____
_____

Sunday Morning Routine: (choose 2 from list)
_____
_____

Create a Daily Morning Routine

(Choose 2 per day from list and this should stay the same each week).

Monday Morning Routine: (choose 2 from list)
_____
_____

Tuesday Morning Routine: (choose 2 from list)
_____
_____

Wednesday Morning Routine: (choose 2 from list)
_____
_____

Thursday Morning Routine: (choose 2 from list)
_____
_____

Friday Morning Routine: (choose 2 from list)
_____
_____

Saturday Morning Routine: (choose 2 from list)
_____
_____

Sunday Morning Routine: (choose 2 from list)
_____
_____

Month: _____

SUNDAY	MONDAY	TUESDAY	WEDNESDAY

THURSDAY	FRIDAY	SATURDAY

Notes

Notes

List of Daily Routines

Having a morning routine assists with developing good habits, which allows us to reach our full potential. Having a morning routine also helps to get rid of distractions and bad habits.

- ✓ Wake up early
- ✓ Meditate
- ✓ Write down 3 things your grateful for.
- ✓ Go Jogging
- ✓ Before you get out of bed Say 3 affirmations out loud.
- ✓ Drink a cup of coffee
- ✓ Don't Get on Social Media
- ✓ Declutter your room/work area
- ✓ Beat your face/ Get glammed up
- ✓ Play your favorite album
- ✓ Make a delicious breakfast
- ✓ Eat a Healthy Breakfast
- ✓ Set 3 short term goals you want to accomplish this week
- ✓ Do/Begin Yoga
- ✓ Make Your Favorite Tea
- ✓ Go get a massage
- ✓ Groom your nails
- ✓ Take a moment to yourself, have a moment of stillness.
- ✓ Speak one affirmation that is the most important to you.
- ✓ Visualize what you want.
- ✓ Write down your affirmation and carry it with you throughout the day.
- ✓ Listen to a podcast about manifesting
- ✓ Paint or Draw your goal/dream
- ✓ Wake up and take a warm bath with a good smelling candle
- ✓ Read a chapter of your favorite book
- ✓ Do your hair and makeup
- ✓ Pray/meditate to calm your spirit
- ✓ Call a friend and catch up
- ✓ Wake up and take 7 deep breaths, in between the breaths say 7 affirmations.
- ✓ If you're religious, read over 7 bible verses that will inspire the day.
- ✓ Spend time with your family and cook breakfast together

- Waking up early automatically puts you ahead of most people productivity wise. It also you gives you more time to include self-care activities.

- Meditation is extremely important for your mind and body. Meditation helps turn negative emotions to positive emotions and can also be a cleanse.

- Starting your day off with gratitude puts you in a better mood throughout the whole day! Even the people around you will have a more pleasant experience being in your presence.

- Exercising is important because it speeds up metabolism, which makes you healthier and it releases endorphins which make you happy.

- Eating a Healthy Breakfast is critical in giving you a clear mind to start the day's activities.

- Saying your affirmation out loud keeps your manifestation goals on track and integral to your miracle.

- Having still and quiet moments helps to center yourself and get to the pureness of who you truly are.

- Visualizing your goals allows you to see them clearly which allows you to achieve them.

Create a Daily Morning Routine

(Choose 2 per day from list and this should stay the same each week).

Monday Morning Routine: (choose 2 from list)
_____
_____

Tuesday Morning Routine: (choose 2 from list)
_____
_____

Wednesday Morning Routine: (choose 2 from list)
_____
_____

Thursday Morning Routine: (choose 2 from list)
_____
_____

Friday Morning Routine: (choose 2 from list)
_____
_____

Saturday Morning Routine: (choose 2 from list)
_____
_____

Sunday Morning Routine: (choose 2 from list)
_____
_____

Create a Daily Morning Routine

(Choose 2 per day from list and this should stay the same each week).

Monday Morning Routine: (choose 2 from list)
_____
_____

Tuesday Morning Routine: (choose 2 from list)
_____
_____

Wednesday Morning Routine: (choose 2 from list)
_____
_____

Thursday Morning Routine: (choose 2 from list)
_____
_____

Friday Morning Routine: (choose 2 from list)
_____
_____

Saturday Morning Routine: (choose 2 from list)
_____
_____

Sunday Morning Routine: (choose 2 from list)
_____
_____

Create a Daily Morning Routine

(Choose 2 per day from list and this should stay the same each week).

Monday Morning Routine: (choose 2 from list)
_____
_____

Tuesday Morning Routine: (choose 2 from list)
_____
_____

Wednesday Morning Routine: (choose 2 from list)
_____
_____

Thursday Morning Routine: (choose 2 from list)
_____
_____

Friday Morning Routine: (choose 2 from list)
_____
_____

Saturday Morning Routine: (choose 2 from list)
_____
_____

Sunday Morning Routine: (choose 2 from list)
_____
_____

Create a Daily Morning Routine

(Choose 2 per day from list and this should stay the same each week).

Monday Morning Routine: (choose 2 from list)
_____
_____

Tuesday Morning Routine: (choose 2 from list)
_____
_____

Wednesday Morning Routine: (choose 2 from list)
_____
_____

Thursday Morning Routine: (choose 2 from list)
_____
_____

Friday Morning Routine: (choose 2 from list)
_____
_____

Saturday Morning Routine: (choose 2 from list)
_____
_____

Sunday Morning Routine: (choose 2 from list)
_____
_____

Month: _____

SUNDAY	MONDAY	TUESDAY	WEDNESDAY

THURSDAY	FRIDAY	SATURDAY

Notes

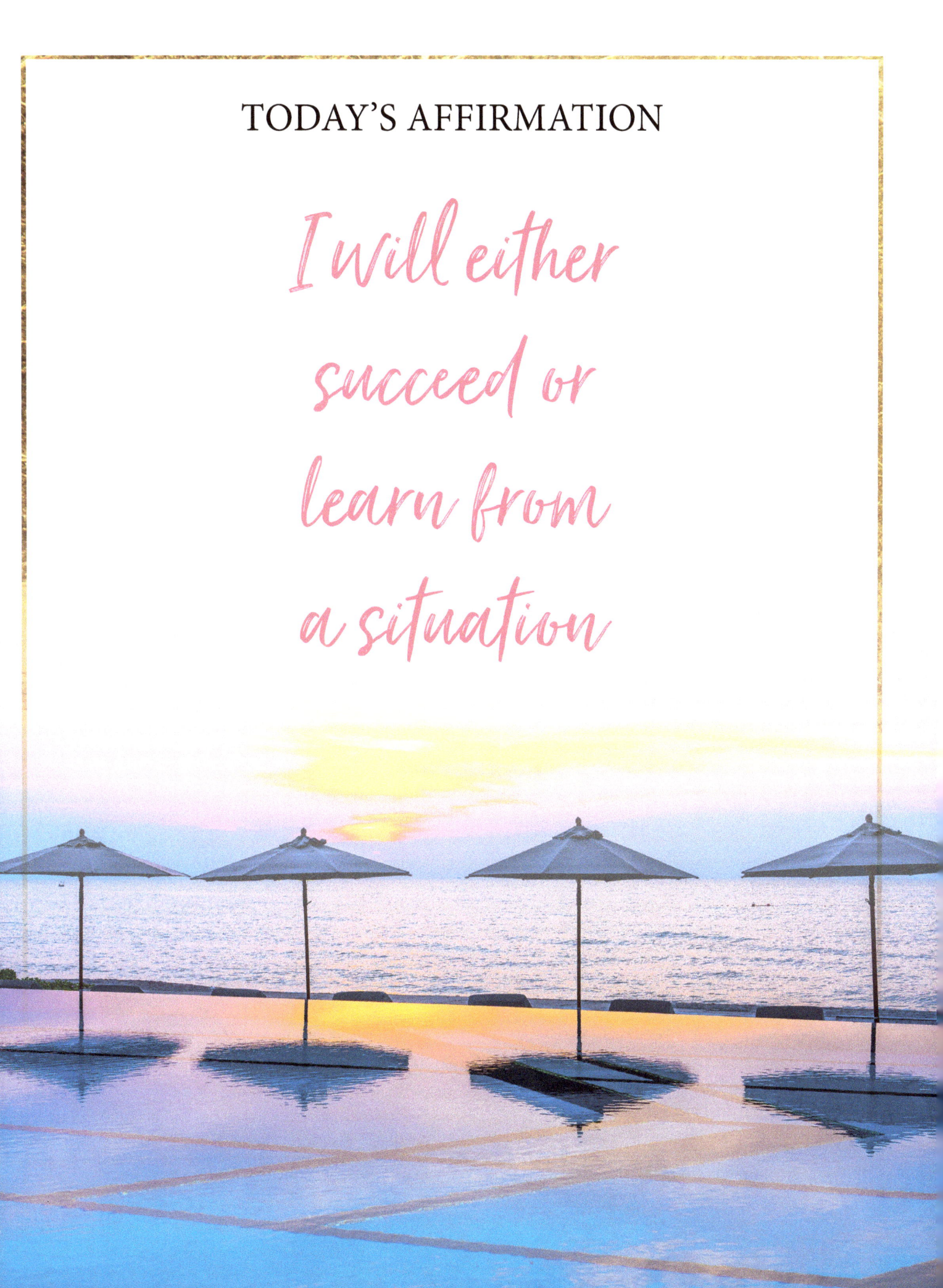

Notes

List of Daily Routines

Having a morning routine assists with developing good habits, which allows us to reach our full potential. Having a morning routine also helps to get rid of distractions and bad habits.

- ✓ Wake up early
- ✓ Meditate
- ✓ Write down 3 things your grateful for.
- ✓ Go Jogging
- ✓ Before you get out of bed Say 3 affirmations out loud.
- ✓ Drink a cup of coffee
- ✓ Don't Get on Social Media
- ✓ Declutter your room/work area
- ✓ Beat your face/ Get glammed up
- ✓ Play your favorite album
- ✓ Make a delicious breakfast
- ✓ Eat a Healthy Breakfast
- ✓ Set 3 short term goals you want to accomplish this week
- ✓ Do/Begin Yoga
- ✓ Make Your Favorite Tea
- ✓ Go get a massage
- ✓ Groom your nails
- ✓ Take a moment to yourself, have a moment of stillness.
- ✓ Speak one affirmation that is the most important to you.
- ✓ Visualize what you want.
- ✓ Write down your affirmation and carry it with you throughout the day.
- ✓ Listen to a podcast about manifesting
- ✓ Paint or Draw your goal/dream
- ✓ Wake up and take a warm bath with a good smelling candle
- ✓ Read a chapter of your favorite book
- ✓ Do your hair and makeup
- ✓ Pray/meditate to calm your spirit
- ✓ Call a friend and catch up
- ✓ Wake up and take 7 deep breaths, in between the breaths say 7 affirmations.
- ✓ If you're religious, read over 7 bible verses that will inspire the day.
- ✓ Spend time with your family and cook breakfast together

- Waking up early automatically puts you ahead of most people productivity wise. It also you gives you more time to include self-care activities.

- Meditation is extremely important for your mind and body. Meditation helps turn negative emotions to positive emotions and can also be a cleanse.

- Starting your day off with gratitude puts you in a better mood throughout the whole day! Even the people around you will have a more pleasant experience being in your presence.

- Exercising is important because it speeds up metabolism, which makes you healthier and it releases endorphins which make you happy.

- Eating a Healthy Breakfast is critical in giving you a clear mind to start the day's activities.

- Saying your affirmation out loud keeps your manifestation goals on track and integral to your miracle.

- Having still and quiet moments helps to center yourself and get to the pureness of who you truly are.

- Visualizing your goals allows you to see them clearly which allows you to achieve them.

Create a Daily Morning Routine

(Choose 2 per day from list and this should stay the same each week).

Monday Morning Routine: (choose 2 from list)
_____
_____

Tuesday Morning Routine: (choose 2 from list)
_____
_____

Wednesday Morning Routine: (choose 2 from list)
_____
_____

Thursday Morning Routine: (choose 2 from list)
_____
_____

Friday Morning Routine: (choose 2 from list)
_____
_____

Saturday Morning Routine: (choose 2 from list)
_____
_____

Sunday Morning Routine: (choose 2 from list)
_____
_____

Create a Daily Morning Routine

(Choose 2 per day from list and this should stay the same each week).

Monday Morning Routine: (choose 2 from list)
_____
_____

Tuesday Morning Routine: (choose 2 from list)
_____
_____

Wednesday Morning Routine: (choose 2 from list)
_____
_____

Thursday Morning Routine: (choose 2 from list)
_____
_____

Friday Morning Routine: (choose 2 from list)
_____
_____

Saturday Morning Routine: (choose 2 from list)
_____
_____

Sunday Morning Routine: (choose 2 from list)
_____
_____

Create a Daily Morning Routine

(Choose 2 per day from list and this should stay the same each week).

Monday Morning Routine: (choose 2 from list)
_____
_____

Tuesday Morning Routine: (choose 2 from list)
_____
_____

Wednesday Morning Routine: (choose 2 from list)
_____
_____

Thursday Morning Routine: (choose 2 from list)
_____
_____

Friday Morning Routine: (choose 2 from list)
_____
_____

Saturday Morning Routine: (choose 2 from list)
_____
_____

Sunday Morning Routine: (choose 2 from list)
_____
_____

Create a Daily Morning Routine

(Choose 2 per day from list and this should stay the same each week).

Monday Morning Routine: (choose 2 from list)
_____
_____

Tuesday Morning Routine: (choose 2 from list)
_____
_____

Wednesday Morning Routine: (choose 2 from list)
_____
_____

Thursday Morning Routine: (choose 2 from list)
_____
_____

Friday Morning Routine: (choose 2 from list)
_____
_____

Saturday Morning Routine: (choose 2 from list)
_____
_____

Sunday Morning Routine: (choose 2 from list)
_____
_____

Am I on track to accomplish the goals I am manifesting?

(If yes what did I do, if no what changes do I need to make?)

_____
_____
_____
_____
_____
_____
_____
_____
_____
_____
_____
_____
_____
_____
_____
_____
_____
_____
_____
_____
_____
_____
_____
_____
_____
_____
_____
_____

Write My Own Affirmation

When you write your affirmations be sure to write them as if they've already shown up in your life! Here are some examples: I LOVE my brand new Range Rover! My new beach home is lavish and beautiful. Perfect for me and my growing family!

_____
_____
_____
_____
_____
_____
_____
_____
_____
_____
_____
_____
_____
_____
_____
_____
_____
_____
_____
_____
_____

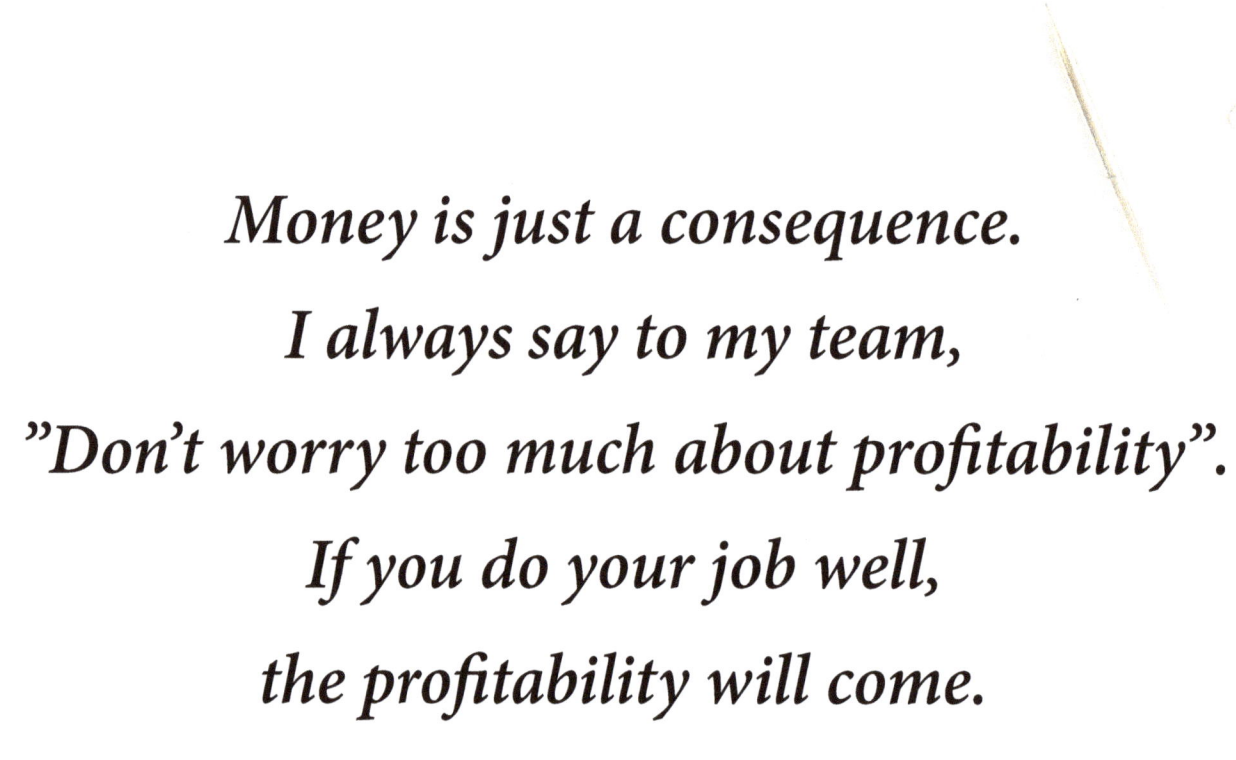

*Money is just a consequence.
I always say to my team,
"Don't worry too much about profitability".
If you do your job well,
the profitability will come.*

BERNARD ARNAULT

The biggest risk is not taking any risk. In a world that is changing really quickly, the only strategy that is guaranteed to fail is not taking risks.

MARK ZUCKERBERG

What Goals Are you Trying to Attain This Quarter?

(A Goal is defined as the object of a person's ambition or effort; an aim or desired result). Here are some examples:
- My goal is to make $10,000 this quarter.
- My goal is to lose 15lbs this quarter.
- My goal is to write a book this quarter.
- My goal is to find a work from home opportunity this quarter.

_____
_____
_____
_____
_____
_____
_____
_____
_____
_____
_____
_____
_____
_____
_____
_____
_____
_____
_____
_____
_____
_____
_____
_____
_____

What steps/action plan do I need to implement these goals?

Here are some examples:
- This quarter I will increase my marketing budget by 10%.
- This quarter I will give up sugar and alcohol.
- This quarter I will spend less time on Instagram and more time writing my book.
- This quarter I will take my free evenings and research work from home opportunities.

What sacrifices do I have to make to achieve these goals?

(Sacrifice is defined as giving up something for the sake of a better cause.)
Here are some examples:
- I will make my coffee at home instead of buying it at Starbucks this quarter.
- I will meal prep and not go out to eat with my friends this quarter.
- I will deactivate my Instagram page this quarter.
- I will leave for work 30 mins earlier than usual so that I can have more time to research new ways to make money from home. I will do this this 3 x a week.

_____
_____
_____
_____
_____
_____
_____
_____
_____
_____
_____
_____
_____
_____
_____
_____
_____
_____
_____
_____
_____
_____
_____
_____

Month: _____

SUNDAY	MONDAY	TUESDAY	WEDNESDAY

THURSDAY	FRIDAY	SATURDAY

Notes

TODAY'S AFFIRMATION

Money flows to me easily

Notes

List of Daily Routines

Having a morning routine assists with developing good habits, which allows us to reach our full potential. Having a morning routine also helps to get rid of distractions and bad habits.

- ✓ Wake up early
- ✓ Meditate
- ✓ Write down 3 things your grateful for.
- ✓ Go Jogging
- ✓ Before you get out of bed Say 3 affirmations out loud.
- ✓ Drink a cup of coffee
- ✓ Don't Get on Social Media
- ✓ Declutter your room/work area
- ✓ Beat your face/ Get glammed up
- ✓ Play your favorite album
- ✓ Make a delicious breakfast
- ✓ Eat a Healthy Breakfast
- ✓ Set 3 short term goals you want to accomplish this week
- ✓ Do/Begin Yoga
- ✓ Make Your Favorite Tea
- ✓ Go get a massage
- ✓ Groom your nails
- ✓ Take a moment to yourself, have a moment of stillness.
- ✓ Speak one affirmation that is the most important to you.
- ✓ Visualize what you want.
- ✓ Write down your affirmation and carry it with you throughout the day.
- ✓ Listen to a podcast about manifesting
- ✓ Paint or Draw your goal/dream
- ✓ Wake up and take a warm bath with a good smelling candle
- ✓ Read a chapter of your favorite book
- ✓ Do your hair and makeup
- ✓ Pray/meditate to calm your spirit
- ✓ Call a friend and catch up
- ✓ Wake up and take 7 deep breaths, in between the breaths say 7 affirmations.
- ✓ If you're religious, read over 7 bible verses that will inspire the day.
- ✓ Spend time with your family and cook breakfast together

- Waking up early automatically puts you ahead of most people productivity wise. It also you gives you more time to include self-care activities.

- Meditation is extremely important for your mind and body. Meditation helps turn negative emotions to positive emotions and can also be a cleanse.

- Starting your day off with gratitude puts you in a better mood throughout the whole day! Even the people around you will have a more pleasant experience being in your presence.

- Exercising is important because it speeds up metabolism, which makes you healthier and it releases endorphins which make you happy.

- Eating a Healthy Breakfast is critical in giving you a clear mind to start the day's activities.

- Saying your affirmation out loud keeps your manifestation goals on track and integral to your miracle.

- Having still and quiet moments helps to center yourself and get to the pureness of who you truly are.

- Visualizing your goals allows you to see them clearly which allows you to achieve them.

Create a Daily Morning Routine

(Choose 2 per day from list and this should stay the same each week).

Monday Morning Routine: (choose 2 from list)
_____
_____

Tuesday Morning Routine: (choose 2 from list)
_____
_____

Wednesday Morning Routine: (choose 2 from list)
_____
_____

Thursday Morning Routine: (choose 2 from list)
_____
_____

Friday Morning Routine: (choose 2 from list)
_____
_____

Saturday Morning Routine: (choose 2 from list)
_____
_____

Sunday Morning Routine: (choose 2 from list)
_____
_____

Create a Daily Morning Routine

(Choose 2 per day from list and this should stay the same each week).

Monday Morning Routine: (choose 2 from list)
_____
_____

Tuesday Morning Routine: (choose 2 from list)
_____
_____

Wednesday Morning Routine: (choose 2 from list)
_____
_____

Thursday Morning Routine: (choose 2 from list)
_____
_____

Friday Morning Routine: (choose 2 from list)
_____
_____

Saturday Morning Routine: (choose 2 from list)
_____
_____

Sunday Morning Routine: (choose 2 from list)
_____
_____

Create a Daily Morning Routine

(Choose 2 per day from list and this should stay the same each week).

Monday Morning Routine: (choose 2 from list)
_____
_____

Tuesday Morning Routine: (choose 2 from list)
_____
_____

Wednesday Morning Routine: (choose 2 from list)
_____
_____

Thursday Morning Routine: (choose 2 from list)
_____
_____

Friday Morning Routine: (choose 2 from list)
_____
_____

Saturday Morning Routine: (choose 2 from list)
_____
_____

Sunday Morning Routine: (choose 2 from list)
_____
_____

Create a Daily Morning Routine

(Choose 2 per day from list and this should stay the same each week).

Monday Morning Routine: (choose 2 from list)
_____
_____

Tuesday Morning Routine: (choose 2 from list)
_____
_____

Wednesday Morning Routine: (choose 2 from list)
_____
_____

Thursday Morning Routine: (choose 2 from list)
_____
_____

Friday Morning Routine: (choose 2 from list)
_____
_____

Saturday Morning Routine: (choose 2 from list)
_____
_____

Sunday Morning Routine: (choose 2 from list)
_____
_____

Month: _____

SUNDAY	MONDAY	TUESDAY	WEDNESDAY

THURSDAY	FRIDAY	SATURDAY

Notes

Notes

List of Daily Routines

Having a morning routine assists with developing good habits, which allows us to reach our full potential. Having a morning routine also helps to get rid of distractions and bad habits.

- ✓ Wake up early
- ✓ Meditate
- ✓ Write down 3 things your grateful for.
- ✓ Go Jogging
- ✓ Before you get out of bed Say 3 affirmations out loud.
- ✓ Drink a cup of coffee
- ✓ Don't Get on Social Media
- ✓ Declutter your room/work area
- ✓ Beat your face/ Get glammed up
- ✓ Play your favorite album
- ✓ Make a delicious breakfast
- ✓ Eat a Healthy Breakfast
- ✓ Set 3 short term goals you want to accomplish this week
- ✓ Do/Begin Yoga
- ✓ Make Your Favorite Tea
- ✓ Go get a massage
- ✓ Groom your nails
- ✓ Take a moment to yourself, have a moment of stillness.
- ✓ Speak one affirmation that is the most important to you.
- ✓ Visualize what you want.
- ✓ Write down your affirmation and carry it with you throughout the day.
- ✓ Listen to a podcast about manifesting
- ✓ Paint or Draw your goal/dream
- ✓ Wake up and take a warm bath with a good smelling candle
- ✓ Read a chapter of your favorite book
- ✓ Do your hair and makeup
- ✓ Pray/meditate to calm your spirit
- ✓ Call a friend and catch up
- ✓ Wake up and take 7 deep breaths, in between the breaths say 7 affirmations.
- ✓ If you're religious, read over 7 bible verses that will inspire the day.
- ✓ Spend time with your family and cook breakfast together

- Waking up early automatically puts you ahead of most people productivity wise. It also you gives you more time to include self-care activities.

- Meditation is extremely important for your mind and body. Meditation helps turn negative emotions to positive emotions and can also be a cleanse.

- Starting your day off with gratitude puts you in a better mood throughout the whole day! Even the people around you will have a more pleasant experience being in your presence.

- Exercising is important because it speeds up metabolism, which makes you healthier and it releases endorphins which make you happy.

- Eating a Healthy Breakfast is critical in giving you a clear mind to start the day's activities.

- Saying your affirmation out loud keeps your manifestation goals on track and integral to your miracle.

- Having still and quiet moments helps to center yourself and get to the pureness of who you truly are.

- Visualizing your goals allows you to see them clearly which allows you to achieve them.

Create a Daily Morning Routine

(Choose 2 per day from list and this should stay the same each week).

Monday Morning Routine: (choose 2 from list)
_____
_____

Tuesday Morning Routine: (choose 2 from list)
_____
_____

Wednesday Morning Routine: (choose 2 from list)
_____
_____

Thursday Morning Routine: (choose 2 from list)
_____
_____

Friday Morning Routine: (choose 2 from list)
_____
_____

Saturday Morning Routine: (choose 2 from list)
_____
_____

Sunday Morning Routine: (choose 2 from list)
_____
_____

Create a Daily Morning Routine

(Choose 2 per day from list and this should stay the same each week).

Monday Morning Routine: (choose 2 from list)
_____
_____

Tuesday Morning Routine: (choose 2 from list)
_____
_____

Wednesday Morning Routine: (choose 2 from list)
_____
_____

Thursday Morning Routine: (choose 2 from list)
_____
_____

Friday Morning Routine: (choose 2 from list)
_____
_____

Saturday Morning Routine: (choose 2 from list)
_____
_____

Sunday Morning Routine: (choose 2 from list)
_____
_____

Create a Daily Morning Routine

(Choose 2 per day from list and this should stay the same each week).

Monday Morning Routine: (choose 2 from list)
_____
_____

Tuesday Morning Routine: (choose 2 from list)
_____
_____

Wednesday Morning Routine: (choose 2 from list)
_____
_____

Thursday Morning Routine: (choose 2 from list)
_____
_____

Friday Morning Routine: (choose 2 from list)
_____
_____

Saturday Morning Routine: (choose 2 from list)
_____
_____

Sunday Morning Routine: (choose 2 from list)
_____
_____

Create a Daily Morning Routine

(Choose 2 per day from list and this should stay the same each week).

Monday Morning Routine: (choose 2 from list)
_____
_____

Tuesday Morning Routine: (choose 2 from list)
_____
_____

Wednesday Morning Routine: (choose 2 from list)
_____
_____

Thursday Morning Routine: (choose 2 from list)
_____
_____

Friday Morning Routine: (choose 2 from list)
_____
_____

Saturday Morning Routine: (choose 2 from list)
_____
_____

Sunday Morning Routine: (choose 2 from list)
_____
_____

Month: _____

SUNDAY	MONDAY	TUESDAY	WEDNESDAY

THURSDAY	FRIDAY	SATURDAY

Notes

Notes

List of Daily Routines

Having a morning routine assists with developing good habits, which allows us to reach our full potential. Having a morning routine also helps to get rid of distractions and bad habits.

- ✓ Wake up early
- ✓ Meditate
- ✓ Write down 3 things your grateful for.
- ✓ Go Jogging
- ✓ Before you get out of bed Say 3 affirmations out loud.
- ✓ Drink a cup of coffee
- ✓ Don't Get on Social Media
- ✓ Declutter your room/work area
- ✓ Beat your face/ Get glammed up
- ✓ Play your favorite album
- ✓ Make a delicious breakfast
- ✓ Eat a Healthy Breakfast
- ✓ Set 3 short term goals you want to accomplish this week
- ✓ Do/Begin Yoga
- ✓ Make Your Favorite Tea
- ✓ Go get a massage
- ✓ Groom your nails
- ✓ Take a moment to yourself, have a moment of stillness.
- ✓ Speak one affirmation that is the most important to you.
- ✓ Visualize what you want.
- ✓ Write down your affirmation and carry it with you throughout the day.
- ✓ Listen to a podcast about manifesting
- ✓ Paint or Draw your goal/dream
- ✓ Wake up and take a warm bath with a good smelling candle
- ✓ Read a chapter of your favorite book
- ✓ Do your hair and makeup
- ✓ Pray/meditate to calm your spirit
- ✓ Call a friend and catch up
- ✓ Wake up and take 7 deep breaths, in between the breaths say 7 affirmations.
- ✓ If you're religious, read over 7 bible verses that will inspire the day.
- ✓ Spend time with your family and cook breakfast together

- Waking up early automatically puts you ahead of most people productivity wise. It also you gives you more time to include self-care activities.

- Meditation is extremely important for your mind and body. Meditation helps turn negative emotions to positive emotions and can also be a cleanse.

- Starting your day off with gratitude puts you in a better mood throughout the whole day! Even the people around you will have a more pleasant experience being in your presence.

- Exercising is important because it speeds up metabolism, which makes you healthier and it releases endorphins which make you happy.

- Eating a Healthy Breakfast is critical in giving you a clear mind to start the day's activities.

- Saying your affirmation out loud keeps your manifestation goals on track and integral to your miracle.

- Having still and quiet moments helps to center yourself and get to the pureness of who you truly are.

- Visualizing your goals allows you to see them clearly which allows you to achieve them.

Create a Daily Morning Routine

(Choose 2 per day from list and this should stay the same each week).

Monday Morning Routine: (choose 2 from list)
_____
_____

Tuesday Morning Routine: (choose 2 from list)
_____
_____

Wednesday Morning Routine: (choose 2 from list)
_____
_____

Thursday Morning Routine: (choose 2 from list)
_____
_____

Friday Morning Routine: (choose 2 from list)
_____
_____

Saturday Morning Routine: (choose 2 from list)
_____
_____

Sunday Morning Routine: (choose 2 from list)
_____
_____

Create a Daily Morning Routine

(Choose 2 per day from list and this should stay the same each week).

Monday Morning Routine: (choose 2 from list)
_____
_____

Tuesday Morning Routine: (choose 2 from list)
_____
_____

Wednesday Morning Routine: (choose 2 from list)
_____
_____

Thursday Morning Routine: (choose 2 from list)
_____
_____

Friday Morning Routine: (choose 2 from list)
_____
_____

Saturday Morning Routine: (choose 2 from list)
_____
_____

Sunday Morning Routine: (choose 2 from list)
_____
_____

Create a Daily Morning Routine

(Choose 2 per day from list and this should stay the same each week).

Monday Morning Routine: (choose 2 from list)
_____
_____

Tuesday Morning Routine: (choose 2 from list)
_____
_____

Wednesday Morning Routine: (choose 2 from list)
_____
_____

Thursday Morning Routine: (choose 2 from list)
_____
_____

Friday Morning Routine: (choose 2 from list)
_____
_____

Saturday Morning Routine: (choose 2 from list)
_____
_____

Sunday Morning Routine: (choose 2 from list)
_____
_____

Create a Daily Morning Routine

(Choose 2 per day from list and this should stay the same each week).

Monday Morning Routine: (choose 2 from list)
_____
_____

Tuesday Morning Routine: (choose 2 from list)
_____
_____

Wednesday Morning Routine: (choose 2 from list)
_____
_____

Thursday Morning Routine: (choose 2 from list)
_____
_____

Friday Morning Routine: (choose 2 from list)
_____
_____

Saturday Morning Routine: (choose 2 from list)
_____
_____

Sunday Morning Routine: (choose 2 from list)
_____
_____

Am I on track to accomplish the goals I am manifesting?

(If yes what did I do, if no what changes do I need to make?)

_____
_____
_____
_____
_____
_____
_____
_____
_____
_____
_____
_____
_____
_____
_____
_____
_____
_____
_____
_____
_____
_____

Write My Own Affirmation

When you write your affirmations be sure to write them as if they've already shown up in your life! Here are some examples: I LOVE my brand new Range Rover! My new beach home is lavish and beautiful. Perfect for me and my growing family!

_____
_____
_____
_____
_____
_____
_____
_____
_____
_____
_____
_____
_____
_____
_____
_____
_____
_____
_____
_____
_____
_____

I believe people have to follow their dreams - I did.

LARRY ELLISON

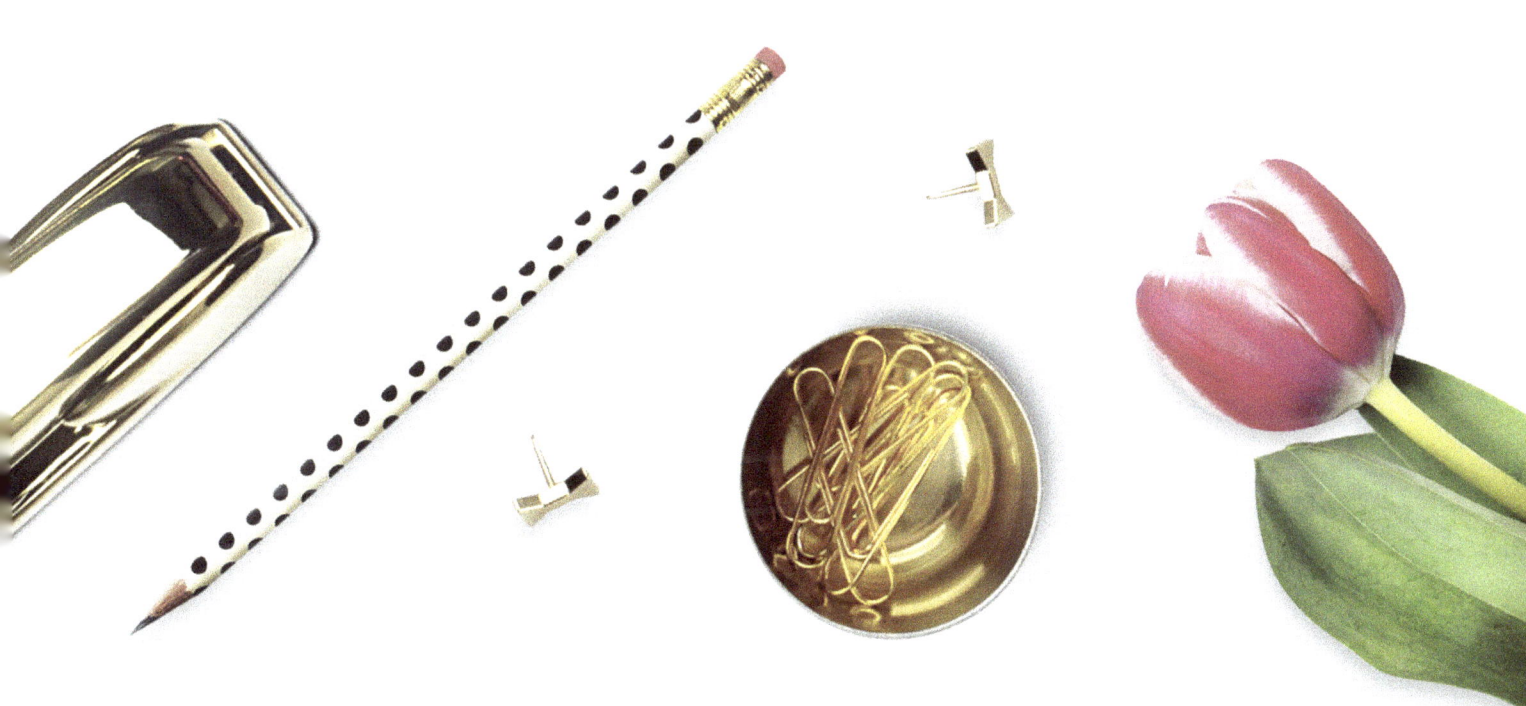

4th Quarter

I'm coming to this world not to work. I want to come to this world to enjoy my life. I don't want to die in my office. I want to die on the beaches.

JACK MA

What Goals Are you Trying to Attain This Quarter?

(A Goal is defined as the object of a person's ambition or effort; an aim or desired result). Here are some examples:
- My goal is to make $10,000 this quarter.
- My goal is to lose 15lbs this quarter.
- My goal is to write a book this quarter.
- My goal is to find a work from home opportunity this quarter.

_____
_____
_____
_____
_____
_____
_____
_____
_____
_____
_____
_____
_____
_____
_____
_____
_____
_____
_____
_____
_____
_____
_____
_____
_____

What steps/action plan do I need to implement these goals?

Here are some examples:
- This quarter I will increase my marketing budget by 10%.
- This quarter I will give up sugar and alcohol.
- This quarter I will spend less time on Instagram and more time writing my book.
- This quarter I will take my free evenings and research work from home opportunities.

What sacrifices do I have to make to achieve these goals?

(Sacrifice is defined as giving up something for the sake of a better cause.)
Here are some examples:
- I will make my coffee at home instead of buying it at Starbucks this quarter.
- I will meal prep and not go out to eat with my friends this quarter.
- I will deactivate my Instagram page this quarter.
- I will leave for work 30 mins earlier than usual so that I can have more time to research new ways to make money from home. I will do this this 3 x a week.

Month: _____

SUNDAY	MONDAY	TUESDAY	WEDNESDAY

THURSDAY	FRIDAY	SATURDAY

Notes

Notes

List of Daily Routines

Having a morning routine assists with developing good habits, which allows us to reach our full potential. Having a morning routine also helps to get rid of distractions and bad habits.

- ✓ Wake up early
- ✓ Meditate
- ✓ Write down 3 things your grateful for.
- ✓ Go Jogging
- ✓ Before you get out of bed Say 3 affirmations out loud.
- ✓ Drink a cup of coffee
- ✓ Don't Get on Social Media
- ✓ Declutter your room/work area
- ✓ Beat your face/ Get glammed up
- ✓ Play your favorite album
- ✓ Make a delicious breakfast
- ✓ Eat a Healthy Breakfast
- ✓ Set 3 short term goals you want to accomplish this week
- ✓ Do/Begin Yoga
- ✓ Make Your Favorite Tea
- ✓ Go get a massage
- ✓ Groom your nails
- ✓ Take a moment to yourself, have a moment of stillness.
- ✓ Speak one affirmation that is the most important to you.
- ✓ Visualize what you want.
- ✓ Write down your affirmation and carry it with you throughout the day.
- ✓ Listen to a podcast about manifesting
- ✓ Paint or Draw your goal/dream
- ✓ Wake up and take a warm bath with a good smelling candle
- ✓ Read a chapter of your favorite book
- ✓ Do your hair and makeup
- ✓ Pray/meditate to calm your spirit
- ✓ Call a friend and catch up
- ✓ Wake up and take 7 deep breaths, in between the breaths say 7 affirmations.
- ✓ If you're religious, read over 7 bible verses that will inspire the day.
- ✓ Spend time with your family and cook breakfast together

- Waking up early automatically puts you ahead of most people productivity wise. It also you gives you more time to include self-care activities.

- Meditation is extremely important for your mind and body. Meditation helps turn negative emotions to positive emotions and can also be a cleanse.

- Starting your day off with gratitude puts you in a better mood throughout the whole day! Even the people around you will have a more pleasant experience being in your presence.

- Exercising is important because it speeds up metabolism, which makes you healthier and it releases endorphins which make you happy.

- Eating a Healthy Breakfast is critical in giving you a clear mind to start the day's activities.

- Saying your affirmation out loud keeps your manifestation goals on track and integral to your miracle.

- Having still and quiet moments helps to center yourself and get to the pureness of who you truly are.

- Visualizing your goals allows you to see them clearly which allows you to achieve them.

Create a Daily Morning Routine

(Choose 2 per day from list and this should stay the same each week).

Monday Morning Routine: (choose 2 from list)
_____
_____

Tuesday Morning Routine: (choose 2 from list)
_____
_____

Wednesday Morning Routine: (choose 2 from list)
_____
_____

Thursday Morning Routine: (choose 2 from list)
_____
_____

Friday Morning Routine: (choose 2 from list)
_____
_____

Saturday Morning Routine: (choose 2 from list)
_____
_____

Sunday Morning Routine: (choose 2 from list)
_____
_____

Create a Daily Morning Routine

(Choose 2 per day from list and this should stay the same each week).

Monday Morning Routine: (choose 2 from list)
_____
_____

Tuesday Morning Routine: (choose 2 from list)
_____
_____

Wednesday Morning Routine: (choose 2 from list)
_____
_____

Thursday Morning Routine: (choose 2 from list)
_____
_____

Friday Morning Routine: (choose 2 from list)
_____
_____

Saturday Morning Routine: (choose 2 from list)
_____
_____

Sunday Morning Routine: (choose 2 from list)
_____
_____

Create a Daily Morning Routine

(Choose 2 per day from list and this should stay the same each week).

Monday Morning Routine: (choose 2 from list)
_____
_____

Tuesday Morning Routine: (choose 2 from list)
_____
_____

Wednesday Morning Routine: (choose 2 from list)
_____
_____

Thursday Morning Routine: (choose 2 from list)
_____
_____

Friday Morning Routine: (choose 2 from list)
_____
_____

Saturday Morning Routine: (choose 2 from list)
_____
_____

Sunday Morning Routine: (choose 2 from list)
_____
_____

Create a Daily Morning Routine

(Choose 2 per day from list and this should stay the same each week).

Monday Morning Routine: (choose 2 from list)
_____
_____

Tuesday Morning Routine: (choose 2 from list)
_____
_____

Wednesday Morning Routine: (choose 2 from list)
_____
_____

Thursday Morning Routine: (choose 2 from list)
_____
_____

Friday Morning Routine: (choose 2 from list)
_____
_____

Saturday Morning Routine: (choose 2 from list)
_____
_____

Sunday Morning Routine: (choose 2 from list)
_____
_____

Month: _____

SUNDAY	MONDAY	TUESDAY	WEDNESDAY

THURSDAY	FRIDAY	SATURDAY

Notes

Notes

List of Daily Routines

Having a morning routine assists with developing good habits, which allows us to reach our full potential. Having a morning routine also helps to get rid of distractions and bad habits.

- ✓ Wake up early
- ✓ Meditate
- ✓ Write down 3 things your grateful for.
- ✓ Go Jogging
- ✓ Before you get out of bed Say 3 affirmations out loud.
- ✓ Drink a cup of coffee
- ✓ Don't Get on Social Media
- ✓ Declutter your room/work area
- ✓ Beat your face/ Get glammed up
- ✓ Play your favorite album
- ✓ Make a delicious breakfast
- ✓ Eat a Healthy Breakfast
- ✓ Set 3 short term goals you want to accomplish this week
- ✓ Do/Begin Yoga
- ✓ Make Your Favorite Tea
- ✓ Go get a massage
- ✓ Groom your nails
- ✓ Take a moment to yourself, have a moment of stillness.
- ✓ Speak one affirmation that is the most important to you.
- ✓ Visualize what you want.
- ✓ Write down your affirmation and carry it with you throughout the day.
- ✓ Listen to a podcast about manifesting
- ✓ Paint or Draw your goal/dream
- ✓ Wake up and take a warm bath with a good smelling candle
- ✓ Read a chapter of your favorite book
- ✓ Do your hair and makeup
- ✓ Pray/meditate to calm your spirit
- ✓ Call a friend and catch up
- ✓ Wake up and take 7 deep breaths, in between the breaths say 7 affirmations.
- ✓ If you're religious, read over 7 bible verses that will inspire the day.
- ✓ Spend time with your family and cook breakfast together

- Waking up early automatically puts you ahead of most people productivity wise. It also you gives you more time to include self-care activities.

- Meditation is extremely important for your mind and body. Meditation helps turn negative emotions to positive emotions and can also be a cleanse.

- Starting your day off with gratitude puts you in a better mood throughout the whole day! Even the people around you will have a more pleasant experience being in your presence.

- Exercising is important because it speeds up metabolism, which makes you healthier and it releases endorphins which make you happy.

- Eating a Healthy Breakfast is critical in giving you a clear mind to start the day's activities.

- Saying your affirmation out loud keeps your manifestation goals on track and integral to your miracle.

- Having still and quiet moments helps to center yourself and get to the pureness of who you truly are.

- Visualizing your goals allows you to see them clearly which allows you to achieve them.

Create a Daily Morning Routine

(Choose 2 per day from list and this should stay the same each week).

Monday Morning Routine: (choose 2 from list)
_____
_____

Tuesday Morning Routine: (choose 2 from list)
_____
_____

Wednesday Morning Routine: (choose 2 from list)
_____
_____

Thursday Morning Routine: (choose 2 from list)
_____
_____

Friday Morning Routine: (choose 2 from list)
_____
_____

Saturday Morning Routine: (choose 2 from list)
_____
_____

Sunday Morning Routine: (choose 2 from list)
_____
_____

Create a Daily Morning Routine

(Choose 2 per day from list and this should stay the same each week).

Monday Morning Routine: (choose 2 from list)
_____
_____

Tuesday Morning Routine: (choose 2 from list)
_____
_____

Wednesday Morning Routine: (choose 2 from list)
_____
_____

Thursday Morning Routine: (choose 2 from list)
_____
_____

Friday Morning Routine: (choose 2 from list)
_____
_____

Saturday Morning Routine: (choose 2 from list)
_____
_____

Sunday Morning Routine: (choose 2 from list)
_____
_____

Create a Daily Morning Routine

(Choose 2 per day from list and this should stay the same each week).

Monday Morning Routine: (choose 2 from list)
_____
_____

Tuesday Morning Routine: (choose 2 from list)
_____
_____

Wednesday Morning Routine: (choose 2 from list)
_____
_____

Thursday Morning Routine: (choose 2 from list)
_____
_____

Friday Morning Routine: (choose 2 from list)
_____
_____

Saturday Morning Routine: (choose 2 from list)
_____
_____

Sunday Morning Routine: (choose 2 from list)
_____
_____

Create a Daily Morning Routine

(Choose 2 per day from list and this should stay the same each week).

Monday Morning Routine: (choose 2 from list)
_____
_____

Tuesday Morning Routine: (choose 2 from list)
_____
_____

Wednesday Morning Routine: (choose 2 from list)
_____
_____

Thursday Morning Routine: (choose 2 from list)
_____
_____

Friday Morning Routine: (choose 2 from list)
_____
_____

Saturday Morning Routine: (choose 2 from list)
_____
_____

Sunday Morning Routine: (choose 2 from list)
_____
_____

Month: _____

SUNDAY	MONDAY	TUESDAY	WEDNESDAY

THURSDAY	FRIDAY	SATURDAY

Notes

Notes

List of Daily Routines

Having a morning routine assists with developing good habits, which allows us to reach our full potential. Having a morning routine also helps to get rid of distractions and bad habits.

- ✓ Wake up early
- ✓ Meditate
- ✓ Write down 3 things your grateful for.
- ✓ Go Jogging
- ✓ Before you get out of bed Say 3 affirmations out loud.
- ✓ Drink a cup of coffee
- ✓ Don't Get on Social Media
- ✓ Declutter your room/work area
- ✓ Beat your face/ Get glammed up
- ✓ Play your favorite album
- ✓ Make a delicious breakfast
- ✓ Eat a Healthy Breakfast
- ✓ Set 3 short term goals you want to accomplish this week
- ✓ Do/Begin Yoga
- ✓ Make Your Favorite Tea
- ✓ Go get a massage
- ✓ Groom your nails
- ✓ Take a moment to yourself, have a moment of stillness.
- ✓ Speak one affirmation that is the most important to you.
- ✓ Visualize what you want.
- ✓ Write down your affirmation and carry it with you throughout the day.
- ✓ Listen to a podcast about manifesting
- ✓ Paint or Draw your goal/dream
- ✓ Wake up and take a warm bath with a good smelling candle
- ✓ Read a chapter of your favorite book
- ✓ Do your hair and makeup
- ✓ Pray/meditate to calm your spirit
- ✓ Call a friend and catch up
- ✓ Wake up and take 7 deep breaths, in between the breaths say 7 affirmations.
- ✓ If you're religious, read over 7 bible verses that will inspire the day.
- ✓ Spend time with your family and cook breakfast together

- Waking up early automatically puts you ahead of most people productivity wise. It also you gives you more time to include self-care activities.

- Meditation is extremely important for your mind and body. Meditation helps turn negative emotions to positive emotions and can also be a cleanse.

- Starting your day off with gratitude puts you in a better mood throughout the whole day! Even the people around you will have a more pleasant experience being in your presence.

- Exercising is important because it speeds up metabolism, which makes you healthier and it releases endorphins which make you happy.

- Eating a Healthy Breakfast is critical in giving you a clear mind to start the day's activities.

- Saying your affirmation out loud keeps your manifestation goals on track and integral to your miracle.

- Having still and quiet moments helps to center yourself and get to the pureness of who you truly are.

- Visualizing your goals allows you to see them clearly which allows you to achieve them.

Create a Daily Morning Routine

(Choose 2 per day from list and this should stay the same each week).

Monday Morning Routine: (choose 2 from list)
_____
_____

Tuesday Morning Routine: (choose 2 from list)
_____
_____

Wednesday Morning Routine: (choose 2 from list)
_____
_____

Thursday Morning Routine: (choose 2 from list)
_____
_____

Friday Morning Routine: (choose 2 from list)
_____
_____

Saturday Morning Routine: (choose 2 from list)
_____
_____

Sunday Morning Routine: (choose 2 from list)
_____
_____

Create a Daily Morning Routine

(Choose 2 per day from list and this should stay the same each week).

Monday Morning Routine: (choose 2 from list)
_____
_____

Tuesday Morning Routine: (choose 2 from list)
_____
_____

Wednesday Morning Routine: (choose 2 from list)
_____
_____

Thursday Morning Routine: (choose 2 from list)
_____
_____

Friday Morning Routine: (choose 2 from list)
_____
_____

Saturday Morning Routine: (choose 2 from list)
_____
_____

Sunday Morning Routine: (choose 2 from list)
_____
_____

Create a Daily Morning Routine

(Choose 2 per day from list and this should stay the same each week).

Monday Morning Routine: (choose 2 from list)
_____
_____

Tuesday Morning Routine: (choose 2 from list)
_____
_____

Wednesday Morning Routine: (choose 2 from list)
_____
_____

Thursday Morning Routine: (choose 2 from list)
_____
_____

Friday Morning Routine: (choose 2 from list)
_____
_____

Saturday Morning Routine: (choose 2 from list)
_____
_____

Sunday Morning Routine: (choose 2 from list)
_____
_____

Create a Daily Morning Routine

(Choose 2 per day from list and this should stay the same each week).

Monday Morning Routine: (choose 2 from list)
_____
_____

Tuesday Morning Routine: (choose 2 from list)
_____
_____

Wednesday Morning Routine: (choose 2 from list)
_____
_____

Thursday Morning Routine: (choose 2 from list)
_____
_____

Friday Morning Routine: (choose 2 from list)
_____
_____

Saturday Morning Routine: (choose 2 from list)
_____
_____

Sunday Morning Routine: (choose 2 from list)
_____
_____

Am I on track to accomplish the goals I am manifesting?

(If yes what did I do, if no what changes do I need to make?)

Write My Own Affirmation

When you write your affirmations be sure to write them as if they've already shown up in your life! Here are some examples: I LOVE my brand new Range Rover! My new beach home is lavish and beautiful. Perfect for me and my growing family!

_____
_____
_____
_____
_____
_____
_____
_____
_____
_____
_____
_____
_____
_____
_____
_____
_____
_____
_____
_____
_____
_____
_____

About the Author

Chelsea is a serial entrepreneur who relocated from Atlanta, GA to Los Angeles, CA, with nothing more than some garbage bags full of clothes, her car and a makeup kit. Determined to succeed in life she went from being a celebrity makeup artist for reality TV shows, to building a 6 figure empire.

Everything Chelsea has manifested has come true. She has dedicated herself to teaching other women how to leave their 9 to 5 jobs by introducing them to the world of drop shipping and e-commerce. Chelsea uses her platform to help transform the lives of those who wish to thrive while spending more time creating memories with loved ones as opposed to conforming to corporate America standards. This journal will help you manifest your dreams and help you accomplish all that is possible so you can reach your full potential.

Interested in Writing and/or Publishing a book? Visit www.A2ZBookspublishing.net

www.ingramcontent.com/pod-product-compliance
Lightning Source LLC
Chambersburg PA
CBHW051347110526

44591CB00025B/2934